Outspoken

poems and short stories inspired by everyday life

Outspoken
poems and short stories inspired by everyday life
16-year Anniversary Edition

Printed in the United States of America
ISBN-13:978-0972787482
ISBN-10: 0972787488
Cover Design by B. Sheldon for B. Sheldon Designs
Back Cover Photo by C. Hauser for Imprint Photography
Studio

Realistically Speaking Publishing Company
10808 Foothill Blvd. #160-260
Rancho Cucamonga, CA 91730

ACKNOWLEDGEMENTS

I thank God for His endless commitment in my life. I thank Him for waking me up at night with words, poetry, songs, creative thoughts, and dreams. I thank Him for motivating me in times when I felt like things were falling apart. God was with me when I was an infant, when my father passed away, and when my mother abandoned me. I can truly say that He took care of me and encouraged me. What better Father to have than the Creator of the universe? He loved me no matter what. He never left my side. He blessed me with a wonderful family - my husband Brian, my son Reginald, and my daughters Jasmyn and Kennedy. No matter how foolish I was, trying to make things happen on my own, God continued to stand with me and teach me. I love you God, thank you for saving my soul.

Brian, you are my example of the love of Christ; you always put God first. It is because of you that I can achieve anything in the world. Thank you for supporting me in all that I do. Thank you for being an excellent husband, father, and friend. I love you very much. Thank you for giving me 26 years of your life. I'm looking forward to many-more.

Reginald, you are blessed with many talents. I'm always encouraged by your drive to accomplish your goals. Stay motivated. I love you.

Jasmyn & Kennedy, you two are awesome! Thanks for helping me with ALL of my projects. I love you so much!

To all of my virtual friendships on Facebook and Twitter: Thanks for all of your comments, "likes", and amazing support.

Enjoy!

TABLE OF CONTENTS

outspoken |ˌoutˈspōkən|

frank in stating one's opinions, esp. if they are critical or controversial.

INTRODUCTION

Outspoken is about the power of truth. Every day is another lesson, and we've all made mistakes that teach us these lessons.

Life guarantees us that mistakes will come, and they will continue to come. No one is perfect, yet some Christians believe they have achieved perfection merely by choosing to follow Christ.

Outspoken is my expression for my own imperfections, and for those who understand theirs. Part of that all-important journey to Christ involves making mistakes along the way, and the more we reveal our shortcomings as Christians, the more we can help and encourage each other as we try to live up to His example.

These poems, short stories, and inspirational sayings are based on everyday situations, whether they are comical or serious. Sometimes we do not admit as Christians how we really feel when we experience these situations, but God says, *"He who conceals his sins does not prosper, but whosoever confesses and renounces finds mercy."* (Proverbs 28:13) God knows our hearts, and *"if we confess our sins, he is faithful and just and will forgive us of our sins and purify us from all unrighteousness."* (1 John 1:9)

The selections included in this book were gathered to reveal what the inner struggle to lead a life with God is like.

Often, we need to be reminded that we journey in the right direction. Life presents us with many trials, tribulations, and tests, but the worst mistake we can make is to reject God as our personal Lord and Savior. He is our stability, our constant source of love and forgiveness, and when we sin we have to recognize that repenting can bring us back into God's favor.

Every Christian falls short of the glory of Christ. Our beliefs are challenged daily, and it is easy to begin to doubt His power. Whether we've erred in word, in deed, or merely in thought, God is the only one who can help us overcome our mistakes.

We are so privileged, to breathe, to sit and stand, to work, and to play. We receive so many blessings, yet we fail to recall the One who is our Provider. Family, friends, finances, all of our gifts of love and happiness, and plenty come from that source. If we can't recognize this, we take life for granted and get lost in worldly concerns.

Recall, however, that this earth is not our final destination. I want to encourage today's Christians to persevere in their efforts to overcome this world, as Christ overcame. He has given us the power to reach that goal. Now we must go into the world, and preach the gospel as we await the coming end and our destinies. These poems and short stories are shared to encourage, inspire, and teach, as you embrace God's gifts and impart His love and forgiveness.

God Bless,

Sheréa VéJauan

MESSY SPIRITUALITY

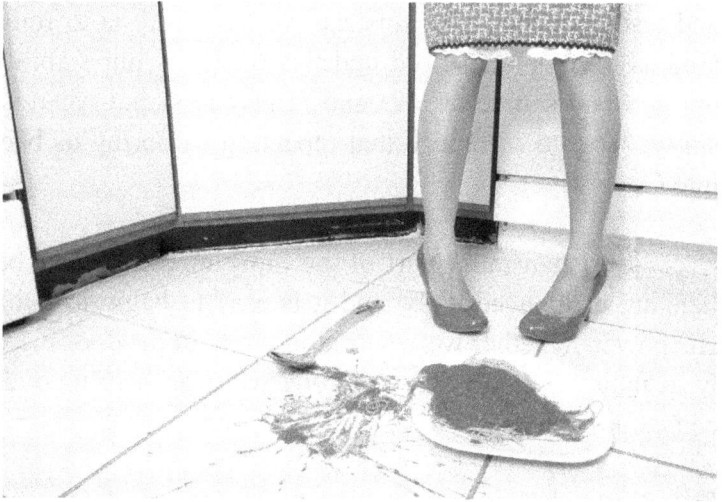

Picture a busy restaurant with customers waiting to be seated, and with people laughing, eating, and drinking. The food is delicious and the conversation is good. Suddenly, a waitress, with a tray full of just prepared plates and clientele that are eagerly anticipating their meals, trips and spills food all over the floor. Everything stops, with the only remaining sound being the echoes of the plates and glasses that just crashed to the ground. Conversations, eating, and drinking ceases while the pleasant faces of people enjoying a night out turn into shocked stares of disbelief.

Immediately she becomes embarrassed. As she tries to recover from the accident, thoughts race through her mind. What will her guests think? Will they be afraid that she will mess up again and spill food on them? Will the other servers be afraid to ask her for help? What will happen to that raise she requested from her boss? When customers come back will they say, "No, not that section please, that girl made a mess the last time we were here." And worse of all, because of what happened, would she now be disqualified from serving?

Well, that is the "real" world, but in God's world He gives us room to make mistakes, even when the whole world stares in disbelief as we make a complete mess out of our lives. We lose friends, we lose support, and people are afraid to trust us again, wondering if we will mess up like the last time.

God, on the other hand sees our messes as opportunities to show off His grace. He rushes over with his towels of comfort and encouragement, His bleach of righteousness, and His sanitizer of love and protection. And as we are still trying to clean things up ourselves He replies, "What mess? I don't see a mess. I don't even remember a mess. Now go in the back, wash up, change your clothes, and get back out there and keep serving." And best of all, because of what happened, we are now even more qualified for service because we are a testament to His grace.

Messy, Messy Spirituality
Does your so-called holy degree
Also give you a license to condemn me?

Yes, it's true;
That out of my life I've made a mess
With every tribulation
I've failed at each test

Having to start all over again
only to confess
That once again I have sinned…
Will I ever live like I'm blessed?

While worldly peers
I've tried to impress, nevertheless
God has come to rescue me with his love
And cleanse me from all unrighteousness

Blind eyes can't see that God is constantly changing me,
Equipping me for the path He's getting ready to take me.
See I messed up, I made a mistake, I admit that I've sinned.
But don't keep denying me and disqualifying me
Cause God has redeemed my sin.

But it's this Messy, Messy Spirituality
That's trying to convince me – and you –
that I'm not worthy
To receive the riches that were promised to me
Riches passed on by my Father
Who in his hands holds eternity!

Now let's be truthful,

I am messed up now
and was messed up then
That's why Jesus took my place and replaced his love on
the cross for my sin
So when God hung his head,
shed blood and died on Calvary
Are you saying he just died for you?
And his blood wasn't enough to cover me?

Oh, ok, now I see…

It's this Messy, Messy Spirituality
trying to convince me
That living for Christ ain't easy
See, sometimes I gotta roll up my sleeves
and let my elbows get greasy
Cause my salvation ain't just for me
But so I can preach to the whole world around me

That the key to not tripping about this mess
Is to understand that with this physical life
comes enduring spiritual tests

And sometimes I may pass with flying colors
But at other times I may fall,
But that's no different than any other
We all have come short at one time or another
So I've learned that when I'm up
I don't give up on my brother.

We all make mistakes, some publicly some privately
But God gave me grace, so I can acknowledge my sin,
Repent and He can restore me

I let others in on the truth so they can see His grace
Not so the whole world would be free to condemn me.

Please understand that I'm not justifying my mess
Or putting the focus on somebody else

I'm just saying I made a mistake and God dealt with me
And I'm going to make more mistakes – but not intention-
ally

Every situation may not be pretty
So I need you to consistently pray that I will be
Always on a journey to where God is taking me

What you need to comprehend
Is that God had my back and he paid for my sins,
And not just for some, but the full amount
So when other folks said I was messed up,
God replied, "No my child, that mess don't count."

*As far as the east is from the west, so far hath he removed
our transgressions from us.*
-Psalm 103:12

THE BEAUTIFUL VALLEY

God is known for explaining His nature in terms of the nature we see around us every day. The Bible talks about "peace in the midst of storms", the "trying and testing of our faith", and also "the valley of the shadow of death." Normally, just the mention of shadows and death are enough to make me want to turn and run the other way – missing out completely on the valley.

But God, in His wisdom, allows valleys in our life to help refine our walk, refill our souls, and to remind us who's really in charge. The valleys have been some of my greatest journeys. They have allowed me to find and define myself. It is the valleys where I learn appreciation and discover who God is to me personally – not just what I've heard from someone else's testimony. It is the valley where I discover my weakness and my hurts in contrast to the strength of my God. I am able to meditate on who he is and the depths from where he has brought me. It is the valley that lets me know my brokenness was only glued – and not fully renewed.

Do you dare to look beyond the barrenness of your valley and see it as something beautiful? Or do you spend so much time questioning God about being there that you miss the blessing of the valley? True beauty journeys beyond appearance and lands at significance.

The valley is beautiful because it shows us that we are so significant and important in God's sight that he would tailor and make valleys to bring us closer to His will.

When I think about my trials, tribulations, and failed tests
Jacked up, slapped up, and in the same ol' mess
Lied on, cheated on, wrong place, wrong time
Crying over a penny cause, I thought it was a dime

I've been laid off, laid down, caught up and disgusted
Tied up, tied down, broke and busted
Then I fell on the floor and hit my head
As I'm looking under my bed, I heard a voice that said

Get up off that floor
Dust yourself off
Thank Me for the good and bad times
Praise Me for the things I have already done
Stop sip-sobbing in yesterday
And start rejoicing for the future
Stop trying to buy a one-way ticket back to Egypt
I have already delivered you from the worst
You are in training for the future
How can you enjoy the green pasture,
Without experiencing the dark valley?

For it is the valley, that makes the pasture green
Praise God for the desert
Praise God for the storm

Praise God for the beautiful valley!

Psalms 23:
The Lord is my Shepherd, I shall not be in want.
He makes me lie down in green pastures,
He leads me beside quiet waters,
He restores my soul.
for His Name's sake.
Even though I walk
through the valley of the shadow of death,
I will fear no evil,

He guides me in paths of righteousness for you are with me;
Your rod and your staff,
they comfort me.

You prepare a table before me
in the presence of my enemies.
You anoint my head with oil;
my cup overflows.
Surely goodness and love will follow me
all the days of my life,
and I will dwell in the house of the Lord
forever.

ONE WOMAN SHOW

Have you ever felt inadequate in the face of other people's talents and gifts? You may have definite skills to bring to the table, but when you look around at what everyone else has to offer, you feel your talent pales in comparison.

I was inspired to write this piece after I received a call from a local performance poetry ministry. They were putting together a poetry concert and they wanted me to be the headliner. I had never heard of a poetry concert, but I had seen the type of poetry that the rest of the poets in the ministry performed.

It was nothing like mine. Their poems usually included dramatic inflections, varied tones of voice, movement, and music. As he told me about the last concert and how he had all of these 'bomb poets' who were 'off the chain' and brought the anointing, I couldn't help but feel like he may have had the wrong number.

My initial thoughts were centered on what I had to offer. "I'm just a poet and a plain poet at that. Maybe he thinks I'm somebody else? I have plain poetry, I don't move, and I don't have any music," I sulked.

I started mentally going through my poems to find the perfect one. God soon interrupted my pity party and spoke clearly to me about the situation. "I haven't called you to do what other people are doing. I called you to just be you," He clarified. Feeling assured that God had created my uniqueness as a poet for a reason, I relaxed and sat down to reflect on what poem He wanted me to present for the event.

So I wrote this piece for that evening, and I dedicated it to all the poets and anyone else who ever felt that their gift may not be enough.

I'm glad you came to see me tonight,
Thanks for coming to my show.
I was so excited
When I saw you coming through the door.

I sent emails to all my friends,
In hopes they would reply.
I know there is plenty you could be doing
On this Sunday night.

I copied flyers and sent out mailers
Cause it's just the right thing to do.
All of this activity
Because I wanted to share some rhymes with you.

Buying tickets in advance
Just to come see little ol' me
I know you want to hear me sing,
Even recite some poetry.

I'm sure glad you could make it
I know you were wondering what I'd wear,
Would I wear a full head weave this time?
Or just decide to do my own hair?

Wow, I'm kinda nervous,
Because this is the big day.
The day I perform for you,
Hope I picked the right piece to say.

I thought I'd bring it like Poetri,
With an amusing twist that's light.
Or maybe I'll go back like The Last Poets,

We can all get revolutionary tonight.

I tried to get up some energy,
To bring it like Maura Gale,
But confidence ain't my middle name
(But when I bring it, I do bring it well)

I tried to bring it like my husband,
Now that dude B. Sheldon is deep.
If I would have brought it like my Grandma
I would have put you all to sleep.

I was thinking about Dr. Ingram,
So maybe I'll give you some history
"Holla back, Africa!"
Or even a piece like 'The Legacy.'

But as God continued to talk last night,
I decided to bring you plain old me

As I went through my poems, books, and poetry cards
Trying to find the perfect piece for you,
I thought
"Wow, this is hard!"

Then it hit me
This is not a show for you,
I'm just a vessel to get God's word through!

So it doesn't matter about the style of my hair,
Or the type of outfit I decided to wear

I can't rack my brain,

To find the ideal piece,
But I can fast and pray,
For God's power to be released.

What matters is the light
I bring with me,
What matters is when God
Anoints this poetry.

What matters is my vow of Christianity
To be a faithful servant
To my God who died for me

So I decided to bring you the God in me,
And just let him have his way.
I decided to pray for you on the way over here,
So at the next concert you'll have something to say.

I decided to lift my eyes to him,
For through him is where my blessings flow.
I decided to give my gift back to him,
And not worry about the next venue or show.

I want you to see me as God sees me,
Cause he loves me very much.
I want you to know how I depend on his love,
And I long daily for his touch.

I want you to know that God opened this window,
So my gift would make room for me.
So I have to continue to open my mouth,
And not worry if you don't like my style of poetry.

I may not write the rhymes like others,
Or groove to poetry beats.
But there is one thing I know how to do,
And that's to kneel at Jesus' feet.

I'm glad you came to see me tonight,
Thanks for coming to my show.
But I have to inform you,
I'm not allowed to perform for folks no more.
Now I play to an audience of one,
So God, this show is for you.
Are you pleased with my performance?
Was I obedient in what you asked me to do?

See God, there's no other star for me,
You have the lead role in this play.
I will always have the best supporting role,
Until my dying day.

There is no other director for me,
You set the stage, you bring the light.
There's no other protection for me,
You encouraged me through the rough nights.

So this right here is a one woman show,
With an audience of only one.
And I hope that God was pleased with me,
But I'm still glad you decided to come.

ETERNAL LOVE

My husband Brian and I were married in 1991. However, in 1997, we separated for about eight months. That was by far the worst thing – and also the best thing – that ever happened to our marriage.

It was that separation that showed me who I was not, and who he really was.

Instead of focusing on my husband's weaknesses, I took inspiration from his strengths.

Instead of focusing on our financial situation, I was awed by God's favor.

Instead of focusing on what we never had, I was able to see more clearly what we had all along.

It was during that time that I really understood that we will never have it all together, but together, we can have it all.

So when we reunited and re-committed ourselves, I made some adjustments to how I would do things from that day forward.

One. I never talk down about my husband in public, or in any group setting, or to anybody. Period. No jokes, no sarcasm, nothing. My husband is always my king, always reverenced and respected. (Now at home and in the car, I might change it up a bit. But I'm still working on that.)

Two. I am always happily married – and everybody knows that. If there is ever a moment when I become unhappy, I only tell two people, my husband and God, 'cause those are the only two that can do anything about it.

Three. I've got three marriage tools: Crisco oil, Clorox, and Midol. Crisco, so I can fry up some good chicken and always keep his stomach full. Clorox, so I can keep a clean home in a peaceful space. And Midol, so I will never say, "Not tonight honey, I have a headache."

In the movies
my daughters see fairytale weddings
I DO
choose you
to live happily ever after

There is no sickness
There's only good health

In the movies
girl meets boy
boy marries girl
carries her off
into the sunset on a white horse

Things only get better
They never get worse

In the movies
the HANDSOME prince shows up
buys the girl a beautiful dress
and one slipper
he truly adores her

No bills, no worries
There is only rich
but never poor

In the movies, they talk for hours on the rooftop
holding each other till morning
they love the same things
they never disagree

There's only sunshine
never rain

But when the movie is over and
after the credits roll
behind the scenes
that's when the real story
starts to unfold

To have and to hold
From this day forward
For better, for worse
For richer, for poorer
In sickness or in health
To love and to cherish
'til death do us part
Love
Eternal love

I mean,
the good, the bad, and the ugliest
unemployment, foreclosure, cancer scares, and stress
childbirth then weight gain, this house is a mess
oh, this is when marriage vows are put to the test

It's behind the scenes
where the greatest lessons are
those I learned from slammed doors
longs walks and
sleeping on the couch

It's when I've opened my mouth
too much for too long and

made a comment where
even my kids say
ouch

It's those behind the scenes where
"nice" mommy is mean
and fried chicken and collard greens
never make it to the table because
I'm not cooking this week
and you know what else I'm doing, right?

But then
I remember that
I do love you

To have and to hold
From this day forward
For better, for worse
For richer, for poorer
In sickness or in health
To love and to cherish
'til death do us part
Love
Eternal love

Not the
buy-me-a-4-karat-diamond-ring-so-I-won't-leave-you love
or being the-best-housewife-in-Atlanta love
or the three-hour-wedding-on-reality-TV kind of love

But the
To have and to hold
From this day forward

For better, for worse
For richer, for poorer
In sickness or in health
To love and to cherish 'til death do us part
Love.
Eternal love

Whenever I'm confused
about my love
I'll remember that

It's the kind of love that makes me
open that slammed door

It's the love that makes me
turn the car around after the long drive

It's the love that makes me
come back after that long walk in the rain
It's the love that makes me
forgive through the pain

It's the love that makes me
get off the couch at three in the morning

It's that love-after-war kind of love

To have and to hold
From this day forward
For better, for worse
For richer, for poorer
In sickness or in health
To love and to cherish 'til death do us part

Love
Eternal love

Now, whenever I get confused about what love is
I look in the mirror and ask myself
Am I patient?
Am I kind?
Am I envious?
Am I angry?
Am I keeping a list of his mistakes?

Because real love
Real, eternal love…

Is patient and kind
Love does not envy
Love does not boast
Love is not proud
Love does not dishonor others
Love is not self-seeking
Love is not easily angered
Love keeps no record of wrongs
Love does not delight in evil
but rejoices with the truth
Love always protects
Love always trusts
Love always hopes
Love perseveres everyday
From this day forward
For better
For worse
For richer
For poorer

In sickness or in health
Until death parts it

Brian, I do love you…eternally!

Love is patient, love is kind. It does not envy, it does not boast, it is not proud. It does not dishonor others, it is not self-seeking, it is not easily angered, it keeps no record of wrongs. Love does not delight in evil but rejoices with the truth. It always protects, always trusts, always hopes, always perseveres. -1 Corinthians 13:4-7

THE RETURN OF MY FATHER WHO NEVER LEFT

R.I.P. William Lloyd Lundy
May 24, 1948 – September 24, 1970

Years ago, I was told my father was killed in a car accident one month after I was born. Well, I found out recently that he was very much alive. I always wanted to know how it felt to have a father, a dad, a pal, a counselor, to walk me through the rules of life, you know, the birds and the bees.

One day to my surprise, I was on my way to a retreat at church. All of a sudden, I became so angry inside. I wanted to know why he had to die before I had a chance to know him? Why did he leave his only child? Why couldn't he drive more carefully? Did he love me when he was here? If he were alive today, would he have left me anyway?

I approached my destination with tears in my eyes, my shirt soaked with tears of pain. A big man with a still voice called my name so clear I knew it was Him. I did not have to ask, I didn't need identification, a physical description, I could hear in His voice. I knew by the way He called my name that He was my Father. "But how could this be, they told me you were dead, but yet, you are very much alive." I began crying and weeping. I was so confused I didn't know if I should be crying or if I should be angry with Him for not finding me sooner. I had so many more questions. "Why did you leave me? Why didn't you search for me? You never provided for me? You missed my wedding and my graduation. But at the same time, I wanted to hug him, I wanted him to just wrap his arms around me and tell me all about his life. I wanted to learn everything about him that I missed out on for years. So I asked, "Where do we start?"

He said first let me tell you my side of the story. "From the very first day you were born your family separated us. They wanted you to believe I was dead; they wanted to hide what we shared together. They wanted to hide the talents that were passed to you. They didn't want you to know how much you resembled me or how we walked the same and talked the same. I was there when you were separated from your family. Somehow I managed to sneak gifts to you... I would leave them in your Sunday school class. I used to come to your church when you were little, singing in the choir. Your spirit was so beautiful and inviting, but the Deacons would not let me in the door. I have always loved you; I was there at your graduation and your wedding. But it was not the right time; I wasn't sure if you were ready. But when I heard you crying, I could not wait any longer. Now you are old enough to make up your own mind, whether or not you want a relationship with me. Your family may not approve, your friends may talk about me, but you have to be ready. I have never, and will never leave you."

I am your Everlasting Father,
A Father of Mercies
And a God of Comfort,
I am Love,
A Wonderful Counselor,
Your Prince of Peace,
I am the Author and Finisher of your faith,
I will never leave you nor forsake you,
I am that bridge that carries you over troubled water
I am the Father to the fatherless,
I am the Lawyer when you need a defense,
I am Peace when you can't be still
I am that raise on your job,
I am that promotion at your workplace,
For if you humble yourself unto Me, I will lift you up,
I am your Light in darkness,
I am your Refuge in the time of trouble;
if you delight yourself in me I
will give you the desires of your heart.
I am He who lives, and was dead, and behold I am alive
forevermore.
Hallelujah!

Yet to all who received him, to those who believed in his name,
he gave the right to become children of God- children born not of natural descent,
nor of human decision or a husbands will, but born of God.
-John 1: 12-13

A LIL' MOUSE IN MY BIG O' HOUSE

I was sitting, chillin', in my big o' house
Then out of nowhere came this lil' mouse
I was so afraid, I ran up the stairs
Stood on the chair, as I wiped my tears

Right before my very eyes
Was the one thing I truly despised
I was not prepared, didn't know what to do
The Bible in one hand, and the other, my shoe

Then..
One day I just cut to the chase
And met that mouse face to face
And by God's amazing grace
I put that mouse in his rightful place

I said to him you are just a lil' mouse
And I'm not gon' let you run my big o' house
I worked too hard to get to this place
Now I'm standing on this chair with a scared looked on my
face

You need to get out and get out today
Before I cheese trap you out of another day
You may have lived here yesterday
But your welcome has been overstayed

I can't serve God in this big o' house
And still be afraid of a lil' mouse
So take yo' little stuff and get out the door
And don't try to come in here no more

I have to make a choice between God and fear
And I choose to serve God all up in here
It took a lot to believe God for this big o' house
And I will not be chased out by a lil' mouse

Thought:
When you get rid of that little mouse, little attitude, little doubt,
little complaining, then you will be ready for the big things.
Faithful in little, faithful in much, Fearful in little is doubtful in everything

A double-minded man is unstable in all his ways

Don't let the little things keep you from the big things God has for you!

ONE MINUTE ON GOD

1 hour 17 minutes on the freeway
Just to go to work

ONE MINUTE ON GOD

26 minutes in the bathroom, reading Wall Street Journal

ONE MINUTE ON GOD

Oh, it's breakfast time; don't forget to slice the fruit, scramble the eggs, cook the meat, bake the biscuits, and squeeze the oranges in the tall chilled glass and then...

ONE MINUTE ON GOD

42 minutes waiting on the #57 bus

ONE MINUTE ON GOD

12 minutes in drive thru, ordering your favorite burger, fries and beverage, "no ice please!"

ONE MINUTE ON GOD

31 minutes, including commercials for your favorite television sitcom

ONE MINUTE ON GOD

5 hours in the beauty salon on Saturday

1 hour on nails, 45 minutes on toes and don't forget the European facial and yet...

ONE MINUTE ON GOD

3 hours at a basketball game, 4 hours on the golf course, 2 hours at the tennis match, but just...

ONE MINUTE ON GOD

2.5 hours on the Internet, 37 e-mails, 5 downloads, chat group (in real time of course) but only...

ONE MINUTE ON GOD

It seems that we will always have forever. But one day, in one second, one moment, in a twinkling of an eye, Our God, He will return and at that moment we will be living in forever, and then it will be too late to ask for...

ONE MORE MINUTE

Find the time for Him, because without Him you would not have any time to give; acknowledge the Time-Giver, the Way Maker, the Bread-Baker.

THE LADY WITH THE WEAVE

I saw her from across the room
My eyes swayed with jealousy
This woman was so beautiful
No one even noticed me
Her hair was long, dark and shiny
Like the tail of a great prize horse
Her personality, and her confidence
Just made the matters worse

The more I watched her as the night passed on
I was convinced, she thought she was all that
The way she swung her hair, round and round
Side to side and front to back
Everyone was standing all around her
hugging her and shaking her hand
She had the attention of everyone
the servers, the guest, and even my man

Finally, I couldn't take it anymore
I had to get a closer look
I needed to get a view of this woman
with whose presence the room was overtook
So I did it, I ran up to her
Then we collided; she said, "Excuse me, are you ok?"
She introduced herself as Serenity,
I said, "Hello, my name is Shay"

She said, "It's nice to meet you Shay
I'll look forward to your prayer"
I wondered what she meant by all that
I just wanted to check out her hair

As I got a little closer,
My eyes could not believe
All of this time I was going insane
And all along this lady had a weave (what?).

I'm all sweating and shaking, angry with myself
Because she thought that she looked so good
But now I see she doesn't compare to me
Although I know she wish she could
Right at that moment a loud bell sounded
She said, "Gather around, it's time"
She took the mic from the podium,
Ms. Grace, Ms. Thang, Ms. Fine

She said "Thank you all for coming
tonight I appeared to be a great dancer.
But as you know this is my going away party
I am rapidly dying of Cancer.
I want to thank God for keeping me full of praise,
Vibrant, healthy and strong
For it is only through Him that I walk with great joy
For His love, mercy and grace has truly shown

I've lost my hair, both of my breasts,
and next I'll lose this life.
But I can hold my head up in confidence,
knowing that when I die I'll die knowing Jesus Christ
So I say to everyone here tonight,
no matter who you are.
Your outer being will shine so bright,
When Jesus is your Morning Star.

I say to those who are struggling,

No matter what you are going through.
With God in your life, His Word in your heart,
He will make your life brand new"
I wept and cried all night long
How stupid of me to sum up this woman's life.
She had to be the most beautiful woman in the world.
Because, If I were in her shoes, I would have never shown
up this night

Thought:

Do not judge a book by its cover,
because between the pages are many untold stories
that cannot be read from the outside.

ARE YOU COMING BACK?

Are you coming back to me?
I long for your return
How long shall I keep your bed warm?
How long should the candles burn?

How long do I look out the window?
Do I save your parking space?
Should I cook your favorite dinner?
Keep this fake smile on my face?

How long do I practice greeting you?
How long do I wait for your call?
Should I play our favorite song?
Are you coming back at all?

I prayed for you to come back home
The Lord answered and said you will
But the way that things are happening
It's hard for me to sit still

I feel so alone
Because you're not around
At night when I am sleeping
I pray to hear the doorbell sound

Wishing you would be there
As I open the door
Praying you'd still love me
Like you did before

I have the Lord deep within,

But there is still room for you
Show me Lord the next steps to take
As I continue to wait this thing through

Question:

Are you still waiting for someone to come back?
A husband, a wife; don't give up, continue to pray; with
God all things are possible.

ARE YOU STILL SAVED ON THE FREEWAY?

I just stepped out of church
Filled with God's Holy Word

As I got on the freeway
There came a big blue thunderbird

Pulled right in front of me
With my kids right there in the car

I started to pull over to the side
And say, "Hey, who do you think you are?

Have you heard of a blinker?
Do you understand the word stop?

Boy, you're lucky my kids are in this car
Or I'd pretend I was Robocop

I'd beat you down like..."

Stop. Hold it. Wait a minute.

Thought:

Isn't it funny how our day can be so wonderful and then we hit the freeway and our entire faith is forgotten about. The freeway could be a very dangerous place both physically and spiritually

So, don't forget to pray. Before you hit the freeway

Don't have anything to do with foolish and stupid arguments, because you know they produce quarrels. And the Lord's servant must not quarrel; instead, he must be kind to everyone, able to teach, not resentful
2 Timothy 2:23-24

AS I HOLD ON TO YOU

As I hold on to you
My life slips through my hands
As I hold on to you
I say goodbye to my man

As I hold on to you
My career becomes past dreams
As I hold on to you
Your plans become my reality

As I hold on to you
A big part of me begins to change
I don't like the same things anymore
My thoughts are re-arranged

As I hold on to you
Those friends I had didn't last
As I hold on to you
My goals start changing fast

Sometimes holding on to God means letting go of...

Everything else!

Thought:

Stop trying to hold on to that lil' bit o' stuff you got, open up your hands so you can grab hold of everything else God has to offer. Please don't choose to be separated from God. Don't hold on to everything else, and let go of Him.

For I am convinced that neither death nor life, neither angels nor demons, neither the present nor the future, nor any powers, neither height nor depth, nor anything else in all creation, will be able to separate us from the love of God that is in Christ Jesus our Lord.
Romans 8:38-39

LOVE - AN ADOPTION LOVE STORY

We think about you every day
And we await the day you will come
We praise God for your existence
From the Lord is where you'll come

We put our trust in only Christ
As we wait to see your face
On the day of your arrival
Truly a vision of God's grace

We can't wait to feel your little hands
And kiss your tiny feet
Your itsy-bitsy baby socks
All wrapped up in a sheet

We can't wait to watch you as you grow
And begin to call us mom and dad
We will thank God for His blessings upon you
Our hearts will rejoice and be glad!

CHRISTIAN

Christian

Christ Like

Like Christ

I am a Christian

I am like Christ

So, tell me Christian…

Are you like Christ?

Or are you just holding a title?

Here is your basic guide to being Christ-like:

*But the fruit of the Spirit is love, joy, peace, patience, kind-
ness, goodness,
faithfulness, gentleness and self-control. Against such
things there is no law.
Those who belong to Christ Jesus have crucified the sinful
nature with its passions
and desires. Since we live by the Spirit, let us keep in step
with the Spirit.
Galatians 5:22-23*

DADDY'S LITTLE GIRL

My Dad is the greatest,
I love Him with my heart and soul

He helps me with my everyday needs
As well as my long-term goals

As I walk down the street with Him
My face is filled with pride

Knowing that my Daddy Jesus
Is walking right by my side!

DARE TO BE DIFFERENT

Dare to take a stand
For what you know is real
Not based on others perceptions
Or on how they feel

Dare to say "Amen"
In a crowd of silent words
Dare to sing your praises
Early like the humming birds

Dare to pray before your meal
While others dig right in
Dare to ask for forgiveness
Admit that you have sinned

Dare to be a representative
For what you know is right
Dare to march with integrity
Do not give up the fight

Dare to believe in the Father
The Son and the Holy Ghost
The Trinity, His Divinity
The one who is The Most

I Double Dare Ya!

I DON'T OWE YOU NOTHING

He said I owed him my life
Because of all the wrong I've done

But...
Jesus said He paid the price
My victory has been won

He said I owed my soul
For the things that I have said

But...
Jesus said it's because of Me
That you are alive and not yet dead

He said I owed him my house
Because of this earthly job I keep

But...
Jesus said I am your Provider
Dry your eyes, no need to weep

He said I owe him my children
Because of my horrible past

But...
Jesus said I removed your sins
Now only what you do for me will last

Look, I don't owe you nothing
You have already stolen enough
I'm hip to your schemes, your tricks, and your plans

I no longer tremble at your bluff

I am under no obligation to serve you
I'm not bound by your decree
Jesus is the one I owe my life to
His death is what paid the price for me!

DO AS I SAY, NOT AS I DO.

My mom had taken a smoke
Not just one, but two
I asked if I could try one
She said "Son, don't do as I do"

She came home late from the party
I woke up at a quarter past three
I asked if I could go with her next time
She said "No, 'cause you'll end up like me"

She had a nice red wine
In a large chilled glass
I asked if I could have a sip
She said, "Boy, the buzz won't last"

I heard her use those words
The pastor called profanity
He said they were not good words to say
So why did she say them to me?

Lord help, I am trying very hard
To do what my mom tells me to do
But I need some type of example
That is why I'm coming to you

In the Bible, you said what you did
And what you did you said it was true
So if my mom is being an example to me
Why does she keep saying don't do as I do?

Thought:

Our children learn from us by what we do,
not what we say. We must lead by example.

Train a child in the way he should go, and when he is old
he will not turn from it.
Proverbs 22:6

EXCUSE MY REACH

I'm sorry if I'm reaching over you
But I'm reaching towards my goal

Pardon me if I pray too loud
But I've got to save my soul

Forgive me if I step too high
But I've got a long ride ahead

Just overlook me if I praise too much
But I'm alive when I should have been dead

I'm sorry if I look too good
But Jesus filled me with His glow

I'm sorry I just couldn't keep it to my self
But it's through Christ all blessings flow

I'm sorry for lifting my head too high
But I realize whose I am

Jesus is my Shepherd
And I am His humble lamb

GET VIOLENT WITH THE VISION!

Get violent!

Knock down doors!

Tear down walls!

Beat up devils!

Kick aside the weights!

Remove the shackles!

Take back what is rightfully yours!

Fight the good fight of faith!

Terrorize the devil!

Spiritually abuse demons!

Get crazy in the Word!

Get bloodthirsty for souls!

Go wild in praise!

Get destructive with God's purpose!

Be out of control in the will of God!

No more silence - only violence!

KEEP STANDING

When you've done all the praying you can do
Keep on praying

When you've done all the fighting you can do
Keep on fighting

When you've done all the standing you can do
Keep on standing

When you have done absolutely everything you could possibly do, keep on doing it.

*Finally, be strong in the Lord and in is mighty power.
Put on the full armor of God, so that you can take your
stand against the devil's schemes. For our struggle is not
against flesh and blood, but against rulers, against the au-
thorities, against the powers of this dark world and against
the spiritual forces of evil in the heavenly realms. There-
fore, put on the full armor of God, so that when the day of
evil comes, you may be able to stand your ground, and af-
ter you have done everything, to stand.*
Ephesians 6:10-13

HELP ME LORD, I'M TRIPPING

Help me Lord, I'm tripping,
On another stupid small thing.
How can I handle the crashes,
When I'm troubled with scratches and dings?

How can you show me the mountain,
When I'm tired from climbing the hill?
If I can't make up my own mind,
How can I do Your will?

How can I inherit your riches,
When I can't even keep a dime?
How can I take care of Your people,
When I can't take care of mine?

Why should I search for a bigger home,
When I'm struggling to pay the rent?
The lights and gas are barely on,
And I'm scraping for fifty cents.

How can I lift up others,
When I can't encourage my own child?
Telling others they should run the distance,
When I struggle with running a mile.

How can I make it to the kingdom,
When I'm dragging to church service on Sunday?
How dare I ask for my own business,
When I am late for work every Monday.

Help me Lord, I'm swimming

In the sea of my past
Help me Lord to understand
That only what I do for You will last
Lord, sometimes the water gets so high,
I'm afraid that I will drown.
Caught up in the loneliness,
Satisfied with feeling down.

The water is in my shoes, my socks
And my shirt is soaking wet
With troubles, worries, material things
And fighting financial debt

Help me Lord I'm drowning
The thoughts are overtaking my soul
Too much thinking, asking, wondering,
Trying to reach my earthly goal

Help me Lord, I'm crying
About what happened yesterday
About what will happen tomorrow
Right now and along the way

Help me Lord, I'm swimming, tripping,
Drowning, crying, dying
I need your help this time
Because I'm sick of trying

Thought:

Often I believe we question God on why, what, when, how, oh yeah, and the why nots. If you believe God is who He is, If you believe that God's Word is true, then no longer must we trip on the past or the present, but we must look to the hills from whence cometh our help. And know that God is not our past help, but He is our present help in the time of all troubles.

Sometimes we do trip, but know that God will always be there to catch our fall.

HEY THIS IS GOD, REMEMBER ME?

Hey how you doin'
This is God, remember me?
I am the one you used to cry to
Down on bended knee

Hey, this is Jesus,
I'd be surprised if you knew my name
I was the one you used to talk to
Before your wealth and fame

Hey, this is Jehovah
The one who set you free
You were bound in the chains of this world
Until you reached out for me

Hey, this is Jehovah Jireh
The provider of all your needs
Now that you're on your own
Your mind is corrupt with greed
Hey, this is...
Forget it
When you are ready, I'll be here

Thought:

When things get rough, we always seem to remember how to get in touch with God, oh but when things are good, we easily forget the one who brought us through. I suggest you use Post-it® note or something, get a safety pin and put notes on your clothes to help you remember who He is and where He has brought you from. Whatever it takes to remember Him… because one thing is for sure. When this life is over, He will say to us,
I never knew you!

HOW COULD I BE SO STUPID?

How could I be so stupid?
Thinking I could out smart you

How could I be so dumb?
Trying to figure out what you would do

How could I be so ignorant?
Trying to change your plan

How could I be so foolish?
Trying to hide from you who I really am

I guess I was delirious
When I thought that I was right

Insane, crazy, senseless
Forgetting you separated day from night

How could I be so stupid?
Trying to walk out on my own

Leaving your glorious presence
When you said you'd never leave me alone

*Are you so foolish? After beginning with the Spirit, are you
now trying to attain your goal by human effort? Galatians
3:3*

HOW MUCH DOES IT COST FOR A MIRACLE?

How much does it cost for a miracle? What amount can I
pay for a clear thought?

What is the charge for some sunshine? How much happiness can be bought?

How much can I pay for contentment? Could I place a
down payment on joy?

Can I purchase a smile or tender moment
To place in the heart of a dying girl or boy ?

What is the price for conception?
I've been trying to have a child

How much does it cost to live longer?
The doctors said I have only a little while

Can I make monthly payments to save my children?
From this sick and cruel world called home

What is the value of a true friend?
Someone who would never leave me alone

Thought:

No matter how much money you may have some things you will never be able to purchase. You can save your money to buy a nice house or car but you will never be able to purchase a loving family or a tender moment, a breath of fresh air, a lil' bit o' sunshine, these things God gives us freely.

Many waters cannot quench love; rivers cannot wash it way. If one were to give all the wealth of his house for love, it would be utterly scorned.
Song of Songs 8:7

I CAN'T BELIEVE I'M IN JAIL

I can't believe that I'm in jail
Not bound in shackles but bound for hell!

I can't believe I'm all locked up
Not with lock & key, but my mind is corrupt

I can't believe I'm incarcerated
Away from the Truth my soul violated

I can't believe that I'm in prison
I've chosen captivity, although Christ has risen

I can't believe I'm behind bars
When I should be free among the stars

I can't believe I'm in slavery
Trapped from the Truth, choosing not to be free

I give up
Jesus set me free
I no longer want to be in slavery

Thought:
Sometimes we lock our own selves up and throw away the
key. Then news gets out that we are in a situation that we
can't remove ourselves from. Our own personal prisons,
but God has provided us with a key called salvation. This
key has the ability to remove us from the prisons of this
world. It starts with prayer; the power that works inside of
us

I DON'T NEED YOU GOD

I don't need you God
Please leave me alone
I don't need you God
I can make it on my own

I don't need you God
I've been making it just fine this far
I bought a brand new house this year
I drive a great big fancy car

I said ...
I don't need you
Why don't you let me be?
Stop sending your little disciples
Over here to talk to me

You see; I'm a good mother, good teacher, and nice wife
I do not need this man, Jesus Christ in my life
I'm not ready for no religion
and I don't wanna be saved

I'll keep on feeling this way
If I have to take it to my grave

If I have to take it to my grave,
If I have to take it to my grave,
If I have to take it to my grave,
If I have to take it to my grave,
If I have to…
(You just might have to do that)

Thought:

Being close to death makes you realize how important life really is.

I WORKED HARD FOR THIS HERE TESTIMONY

I went through hell and high-water
I went through abortions, miscarriages
Marriages, divorces
Drugs, alcohol, prostitution
Selling my soul to the devil through Tarot Cards,
Astrologists, Cleo telling me my future (joke)

I tell you I worked very hard for this here testimony
I went through unemployment, self-employment
And no employment
Physical abuse, substance abuse, sexual abuse, mental
abuse, family misuse

I went through church, no church,
picked the wrong church, left that church
went through jail, gangs, and other stupid thangs
went through long hair, short hair, no hair, bad hair day
(you know what I'm saying)

But through all these things, the Lord God made a way for
me to escape and He gave me this here testimony.

I am a living, walking, breathing, singing, and praying tes-
timony. You might break into my house and take some
stuff, you might lay me off my job but one thing I will al-
ways have with me wherever I go is this here testimony,
testimony of assurance, testimony of deliverance, testimo-
ny of overcoming, testimony of faith, testimony of grace,
testimony of courage.

The world swallowed me up; the devil spit me out

my spouse kicked me out; my kids cussed me out
But Jesus brought me out, and this here is my testimony.

LAST NIGHT I LET THE ENEMY MAKE LOVE TO ME

Last night I let the enemy l make love to me
He whispered in my ear
Let me show you how I can love you
There is no need to fear

No matter what you've heard about me
I will do your body right
I know just what you're thinking
I know exactly what you like

I have committed my life to study you
So I would know just what you need
He knew about my past
My parents, and their seed

He knew about my family, my friends
And even my deceased dad
He was so irresistible!
The best man I have ever had

He knew my favorite color
He smelled of my favorite scent
Before I could say anything at all
He already knew what I meant

I felt so secure with him
It was as if he knew me all the time
I lay awake in his arms
As he poured the perfect wine

He kissed me with his lips of deception
And his tongue of constant lies
The breath of endless nightmares
The sparkle of death was in his eyes
His foreplay was superb
He enticed me all night long
At times I wanted to break away
But his power over me was too strong
And then...

I remember waking up in the morning
To find that he was not there
How could he leave my house in such a mess?
I thought he said he cared

He stole my cash, my car, and my dreams
In exchange for just one night
How did I let this happen to me?
How did I lose my sight?

How could I give up my body
My mind and my soul?
How did I walk such a straight line
To end up in a black hole?

Thought:

While we may not want to admit it, we spend time with the devil. We let him seduce us with his charm. We let him flirt with us, his magnetic flow becomes so irresistible, and we allow him to violate us with his smooth talking. We allow him to whisper sweet nothings in our ear. He approaches us as if he knows us so well; we began to feel secure with him. We take him to work with us and bring him back with us and invite him into our home to meet our children, and our spouse. Then all of a sudden we wake up one morning trying to act like we didn't know we were being tricked (yeah right) (save the drama),God says resist the devil and he will flee. The devil only has as much power as we allow him to have. We have the power over our own tongue in the way we communicate to others. We have the power over the mates we choose to join ourselves with. We have the power over the way we behave at work.

WE HAVE THE POWER! AND DON'T EVER FORGET IT!

MY SECRET LIFE

My job don't know

My family really don't know

Definitely can't tell my friends

Don't you dare mention this to my kids

Here it goes:

In my other life

I'm really a Christian

SHHHHHHH don't tell anyone

Let's just keep this between us.

OOPS, I FORGOT TO PRAY!

Oops, I forgot to pray!
To lift my hands and thank the Lord for this day

I forgot to get on my knees and thank Him for his grace
I forgot to give Him praise as I fall down on my face

I forgot to lift my voice to praise His Holy Name
To come into His presence there's no one quite the same

Oops, I forgot to pray
But He is so forgiving; He blessed me any way

PEACHES AND CREAM

Oh just because you are a little Christian now
You think everything is supposed to be

Peaches and cream

Black and white

Honky Dory

La di da

Happy go lucky

Not?

Let me tell you this; trials, they do come, but they only come to make us strong; take the test, conquer it, and move on Oh yes there are good times and the good times come when you have joy in the midst of sorrow and Jesus is that joy. I'd rather be going through trials with God than without Him. And if you are not going through struggles maybe you are not worth the devil's time (Hmmm) make it a point to be the devil's enemy, make him hate you, make him despise you. He should be trying to attack you every chance he gets. 'Cause if he ain't messing with ya, then ya ain't worth messing with.

PISS ME OFF, WHY DON'T YA

You should have seen my face when that fool took my parking space, you knew I was getting ready to park there, I waited for that lady to pack all her groceries in there, put the kids in the car, and then out of nowhere here you come.

First, you left me on hold for fifteen minutes, then you hung up in my face, nobody hangs up in my face, oh, I am really pissed off now,

You took my husband, after I helped him get through school, and cooked breakfast every morning, took care of the kids, just wait until I get my hands on you girl

You stole my idea, which was my idea, I am very pissed now you took my job, I was supposed to get that job, just don't let me find out where you parked your car

I'm so mad, if one more person, does one more thing to me today it is on and cracking cause, I am pissed off

Thought:

Well if that little stuff got you mad, I guess you really would have been pissed off, if you would have been cruci-fied for someone else's sin

Oh, how I thank you for not being my Savior
'Cause if you were my Savior

Then I would have really been pissed off!

SURE, I SPEND TIME WITH GOD

Sure, I spend time with God
Each and every day
But not before I comb my hair
And not before I plan my day

Well I do spend time with God
Maybe not every, every day
Of course not before the football game
'Cause I gotta see my boys play

Sure, I spend some time with God
Each and every hour
But not before I pay my rent
My food & department of water & power
('Cause you know they will cut yo' stuff off)

Sure, I spend a little time with God
Each and every minute
But not before I make plans for my house
And of course, what I'll need to put in it

Sure, I spend time with God
Whenever I get a chance
But not right now my song is playing
And you know I've got to dance

Oh yeah right I spend time with God
I mean what is time anyway, just a number
He can wait for me whenever I'm ready
Because he never sleeps or slumbers

Thought:

After everything is said and done: How much time
do you really spend with God?

THOSE WERE THE DAYS

I went to church and shook the preachers' hand
But I was never introduced to Jesus Christ the man

Pretty ruffled socks and patent leather shoes
But I never learned to obey the Church rules

I remember the crumpled crackers and the purple juice
But I never knew I had the power to say: "Satan turn me loose"

Sang in the choir but never learned to praise,
Just a church goer, not a seed sower, oh those were the days

HE MADE ME DO IT

He made me do…
Whatever it took to reach my goal
He took care of all my needs
And then he took my soul
He made me trip
But God, turned on the light
God told me to pray
He said let's fight

The devil made me want that man
I saw with lustful eyes
The devil made me party all night long
You know how time can fly
The devil made me hit that car
And then run so fast away
The devil made me take that dress
'Cause I didn't have enough to pay

The devil made me skip Sunday service
By keeping me out all Saturday night
Though Jesus said don't eat the fruit
The devil said, it won't hurt, just take a little bite
The devil made me drop out of school
By making my work too rough
The devil made me leave my spouse
Because the income was not enough

The devil told me to tell you off
The Lord said to speak in peace
The devil made me quit my job,
My boss was just too mean to me

Now I am back in the prayer line again
Praying about what the devil made me do
God said, I am sorry to break the news today
But I believe that all along that devil was you

Submit yourselves, then, to God. Resist the devil, and he
will flee from you
James 4:7

THE ENEMY TRIED TO TAKE MY SOUL

The enemy tried to take my baby
Late in the midnight hour
The enemy tried to take my mind
And release me from God's power
The enemy tried to steal my soul
And leave me out for death
The enemy tried to take my heart
He tried to take my breath

The enemy tried to steal my family
One by one
The enemy tried to take my victory
I believe he thought he'd won
I tried to fight back in my dreams
But my voice would not proclaim
All I could do is fight in my spirit
And call on Jesus name

I had to hang in there no matter what
I'd fight the battle through
Realizing that the very next day
The Lord would have a greater work for me to do
I prayed the Lord would use me
To fulfill His Holy Will
I knew that there would be warfare
And at the enemy's price, I'd pay the bill

As I slept my way to daylight
My eyes were opened wide
I knew that God had visited me
And placed more gifts inside

I'd conquer one more night of wrath
And one more day of grace
I'll have many more opportunities
To talk to God face to face
But one thing, during this struggle,
I will never forget
Jesus has kept me this far
And he has not failed me yet

THE LORD'S DAY, LIVIN' IT THE LORD'S WAY

The Lord's way is my way
The Lord's hope is my hope
This is the day the Lord has made
The Lord's strength is my dope

The world's work is not my job
The world's money is not my keep
The world's house is not why I live
The world's source is not what I seek

The Lord's ministry is my work
The Lord's tithe is what I sow
The Lord's heaven is where I'll live
The Lord paid the debt I owed

The world's time is not my time
The world's dress is not my style
The world's dream is not my goal
The world's child, that's not my child

The Lord's armor is my dress
The Lord's time is my time
The Lord's will, is my desire
The Lord's child, oh yes, he's mine

As I live in the world today, I must remind my self that although I live in this world,
I am most definitely not of the world. Therefore the world's way of life is not my life
nor is it my lifestyle; but my life is in, for, of and because of Jesus Christ,
my God, my Savior, Healer and Provider and in true living I must live the Lord's day the Lord's way.

Do not conform any longer to the pattern of this world, but be transformed
by the renewing of your mind. Then you will be able to test and approve what
God's will is, his good, pleasing and perfect will.
Romans 12:2

Do not love the world or anything in the world. If anyone loves the world, the love of the Father is not in him.
1 John 2:15

THE PART THAT'S NOT FAIR ABOUT PRAYER

You asked me to pray that your life would be right
But yet, you still party every night

You asked me to pray for the healing of your body
But you did not say you smoked dope at the party

You asked me to pray for the repentance of your sins
But right after prayer, you go sin again

For I am your friend and I would love to pray with you
But there are some things I need you to do

I need you to agree, believe and repent
So I can know in my heart, our prayer will be heaven sent

If we deliberately keep on sinning after we have received
the knowledge of the truth, no sacrifice for sins is left
Hebrews 10:26

Again, I tell you that if two of you on earth agree about
anything you ask for,
it will be done for you by my Father in heaven.
Matthew 18:19

THE REHABILITATED MAN

Not made over
Made up
Covered up
But a new creation in Christ Jesus
My slate is clean
My convictions erased,
Sin's tossed as far as the east is from the west
There is not a file cabinet with my sins in it.

No, I am not a rehabilitated man, but I am a brand new man. Old things have been past away and everything about me is now new.

Hallelujah!

THIS WORLD

This world was created with "Let there be…"
By "I am" who is to come!

This world was tricked by vanity
The vile and evil one

Jesus Christ saved this world
His blood was shed for all

This world was doomed by lucifer
The day he took that fall

This world was loved by the Father
Who gave His only Son

This world is hate; it's lust, its strife
One day it will all be gone

The world and its desires pass away, but the man who does
the will of God lives forever.
1 John 2:17

THREE SOLID WAYS TO AVOID HELL

The Father

The Son

The Holy Ghost

WHAT IF THERE IS NO GOD?

Where is the light switch for day and night?
Where is the timer for the sun and the moon?
Where is the sprinkler for the rain?
Where is the expiration date printed for human life?

A fool has said in his heart there is no God

WILL YOUR WEALTH REPLACE ME?

Will your wealth replace me,
The child I love so much?

Will your money buy a massage,
Where you will no longer need my touch?

Will your riches buy you sweet music,
Where there is no joy in praise?

Will your fortune buy you a position,
Where your confidence is raised?

Will your resources buy you food and drink,
Where you will no longer thirst for me?

Will prosperity make a way for bail,
Where the Father cannot set you free?

Thought:

Money, assets, resources, riches, fortune, prosperity, abundance, these are all words that we are familiar with. But on the day of the God's return these very words will mean

NOT ONE SINGLE THING!

But remember the Lord your God, for it is he who gives you the ability to produce wealth, and so confirms his covenant, which he swore to your forefathers, as it is today.
Deuteronomy 8:18

WORK VS. GOALS

Work is a place where you spend most of your day
doing what you don't want to do

Goals are something that you don't have time for
because you are too tired from working

If you did not work
then you would have more time for your goals,
and the things you want to enjoy

But if you strived on achieving your goals without working
you would not have enough money to support the goals
that you have.

Hmmm...

Solutions:
Be someone who is rich
or
Have a Father who is

With me are riches and honor, enduring wealth and pros-
perity
Proverbs 8:18

THE CHURCH HALLWAY

Standing in the church hallway
Deciding if I should go in

Saddened at my life
Afraid of all my sin

See the people passing me
Not to speak a word

As Jesus whispers in my ear
Like a small bird

Inside the church are others
Hurting just like you

Some still not fulfilling the purpose
I have called them to do

Waiting on another
to fulfill my will

In the meantime souls are hurting
While my ambassadors are standing still

Please walk through that door, don't you wait another day

Don't be afraid my child,' cause I'll be with you all the
way

WILDERNESS PAIN

I'm taking a trip to the wilderness
Don't know how much time it will take

Gotta go through some thangs to get some thangs
Gotta make some mistakes

Enduring the pain of the promise
Whatever it takes to fulfill His will

Traveling with my one bag of loneliness
Everything else I need God will fill

"Endure the pain of the promise"

MY VIEW

I thank You for the view, I have of You

The way I've changed, all that I do

My heart and soul are now brand new

Although you have called many

I'm glad to be of the chosen few

CONVERSATION

This is you:
God I'm gon' help you out

This is God:
No thanks; you have already messed up enough

Just be still and know that I am God

GET UP

"Lord I've fallen
and
I can't get up"

So you fell, get up and start over again

We are hard pressed on every side, but not crushed; per-
plexed, but not in despair; persecuted, but not abandoned;
struck down, but not destroyed
2 Corinthians 4:8-9

ALL LOCKED UP

Don't think you've got it all locked up
Things change
People change
Circumstances change
Finances change
Jobs change
Addresses and phone numbers change
Attitudes continually change
Even hair color changes from time to time
Now, you know your friends keep changing

But hallelujah!
I know someone who never changes

For the Lord God never changes

> *I the Lord do not change.*
> *Malachi 3:6*

DESIRES

And God Says…

Oh yes,
I will give you the desires of your heart,
but when your desire becomes greater than Me
then we have a problem

FALL ON MY FACE

Just imagine the things that would have taken place
If I had failed to fall on my face

Just imagine the heartache that time erased
All because I fell on my face

When I was in trouble, the Lord pleaded my case
Because I never forgot to fall on my face

In order for me to continue this Christian race
I can never, ever forget to fall flat on my face

MY HELP

Am I trusting in my self,
To get me through the day?

Or trusting in my help,
As I begin to pray?

                    Jesus is my help!

SECOND-HAND SMOKE
(It could really kill ya)

Don't let second hand smoke,
get you a first class ticket to hell
Don't let your friend's sin,
get you your own private jail cell

Don't let others' vision,
cause you to loose sight of your own
Don't let this temporary wealth on earth,
rob you of God's throne

Do not be misled: Bad company corrupts good character.
1 Corinthians 15:33

LORD, STOP CALLING ME!

He just kept calling
And calling
And calling
And calling
And…

Finally I picked up the phone and said, "Yes, Lord".

And what a joy it is to be in the will of the Lord.

When God calls, please answer

For many are called but few are chosen
No, let me rephrase that
God calls many
But few answer the call

Please answer, before He stops calling you
Share your gift with the world

STICKS AND STONES

Sticks and stones
Do break your bones
But eventually they'll heal

But names and thoughts
And people talking 'bout you
Eventually become real

(If you let it)

TOMORROW

Tomorrow…
I may have some dreams of doing many other things.

But today…
I need to keep this gig and make it work.

MIRROR, MIRROR

Mirror, Mirror what do you see?
I see someone who looks like me
I mean this is my hair, my face, my hat
But I can't tell where my soul is at

Mirror, Mirror look again
God has already forgiven me of that sin
But every time I look at you, you show me again
The past I thought had come to an end

Mirror, Mirror here I am
I've been purified by the Blood of the Lamb
The next time you look at me
My inner man is what you'll see

Mirror, Mirror your such a Liar
I have been redeemed by the Father

CAN YOU HANDLE IT?

Your eyes have not seen
and your ears have never heard
the things that God has already prepared for you
So, stop complaining and start preparing
Get ready, 'cause you ain't ready

Can you really handle what you are asking God for?

LORD I'M SCARED

Lord, I'm scared to take that walk
To make that jump
To make that change

Afraid to move ahead
To step back to rearrange

I'm terrified of my new life
My new dreams and my goals

I'm scared of my today, my tomorrow,
and what my future holds

And God Says:
"Don't be afraid, I am always with you"

DON'T WASTE MY TIME

Girl don't waste my time
Talking about who you are

How you are the bomb
And gon' be a movie star

Girl don't waste my time
Showing me all your stuff

I don't care about that
And I have seen more than enough

I know whose I am
And I know where I'm going

I'm secure in where I stand
Rain, sleet or snowing

So, go tell somebody else
Who shares joy in your pride

I built my character in Jesus
And my strength comes from inside

COMPLETE SELF-DESTRUCTION

Complete Self-Destruction

Is

Being a hearer only and not a doer

But the one who hears my words and does not put them
into practice is like a man
who built a house on the ground without a foundation. The
moment the torrent struck
that house, it collapsed and its destruction was complete.
Luke 6:49

I CAN'T DO IT

I don't know when he's going to do it
Or how he'll get me through
All I know is that in my strength
There's no more I can do

There's no one I can call for this
I am not set up with earthly wealth
There's no one who can fix this thing
But Jesus Christ himself

There's no door I could walk through
No shortcuts I could take
All I can do is trust in him
'Cause my whole life is at stake

There's no window I can climb through
Or backstairs alley way
There's no dialogue I can practice
No short sweet words to say

I'm stuck I'm through, Lord here I am
Please, just have your way
I have no more plans, solutions, or schemes
Your way, it starts today

Remembering daily:

It is not I, but Christ who lives inside of me

SEE THAT WAS THE PROBLEM IN THE GARDEN

I think we all have bitten a few apples
But everybody wanna talk about Eve
About how she was deceive
The garden scene was too hard to believe
They say she ate her family out of house and home
I say she did not eat by herself,
Adam let his wife walk out alone

He probably was watching the football game
And said you go right on and get me some food
You know, legs on the table, drink in hand,
Not paying attention, being rude
He said it was that woman you gave me
Yeah, her name was Eve
With that smooth sweet voice, soft legs, curved hips
And that long dark hair weave

God if you had never given her to me
This situation we would not be in
Now we all have to move, short on food,
All because of that woman's sin
That woman made me do it
Then she said no it was not me
It was that serpent you created
That met me at the tree

Stop, stop, stop

Men, stop blaming your wife
Women, stop blaming that snake

Take some responsibility of your own
Please, for goodness sake
See the problem was not her, him, or the serpent
Can't you see?
God wanted someone to admit
Hey, it was me

Thought:

You don't have to take the blame to accept the responsibility, Let us be responsible for our own actions and leave Eve alone. What happened in the garden, was in the garden. Where are you at right now?
Who are you listening to now? Who is deceiving you now?
Who is responsible for your sins now?

CLOUDY DAYS

Even though it may look cloudy outside

The "Son" is still shinning

We must thank God for every day we have the opportunity to wake up this is the day that the Lord has made, all you need to do is be glad and rejoice

DEVASTATION REVEALED

Total devastation revealed
While my abundant blessings remain concealed

Don't know what to feel
Can't tell if it's real

I asked the Lord to heal
All the pain inside I feel

The enemy he didn't reinvent no wheel
He's always come to destroy, steal, and kill

Ever since we were given free will
We had our own set of cards to deal

Oh the enemy, he is real
But my God is the one who gives the final seal

A SONG IN MY HEART

Jesus put a song in my heart
On the freeway
In the line at the grocery store
Standing in line at the bank while I'm making a deposit
At my cousins birthday party
Walking through the park
I had to keep it to myself
didn't want nobody to think I was c-ra-zy (ya know)

I was in the mall
And finally I realized I was blessed
I mean truly blessed
My spirit started jumping
Tears flowing down
I had to dry my eyes quick
Or I would have found my self being led out in the "white jacket"

I can't believe all of the things the Lord has done for me
But when I think of his goodness
My heart starts singing all over again
And again
And again
And again
And again

LIVE NOW

Live now, die later
Die now, live later

It's not about you
It's all about Jesus

To live, is to die
To get, is to give

To love, is to hate sin
To hold on, is to let go

Live now, die later
Die now, live later

We have two destinies
Life and death
Choose how you will live both

PRO-CHOICE

Pro Choice
Right to choose
God gave me a voice
No way out of Pro-Choice
God is Pro-Choice
God allows us to choose, always has
Doesn't mean that your choice is right
Just ask Lucifer, He made a choice
We must abort death in order to choose life
Be pro-Choice
But choose right
Choose life
Life is Christ

Choose today whom you will serve.

IF GOD?

If God be for you
Then who…
Then what…
Then why…
Then how…

One more time
If God be for you,
Then, what person?
What job?
What disease?
What circumstance could ever be against you?

Do not be defeated; know whose you are

I'M BLESSED BUT DEPRESSED

I'm blessed but depressed
So sick of this mess

The enemy warrants my arrest
As he seeks to mutilate my flesh

Although I had on my breast plate of righteousness
They still found cancer in my left breast

Only got a few months left
God, is this another test?

Trying to fight my best
If only I could rest

I shall look upon the Lord
And on him my eyes will rest

Constantly being challenged, neglected
And on every side, hard-pressed

Totally being convinced
That I could never be blessed

No longer will I be depressed,
'Cause if I'm still alive, then I must be blessed

Thought:
Everything that is bad, May not be the worst

TRUST

I was gon' trust in the Lord
With all my heart
And all my soul
And all my mind
But then…
I decided to lean on my own understanding

*Trust in the LORD with all your heart
and lean not on your own understanding;
in all your ways acknowledge him,
and he will make your paths straight
Proverbs 3:5-6*

CASUAL CHRISTIAN

I've spent my whole life
Growing up in the church
And I've seen that none of this prayer stuff really works

So why should I waste time on this type of decision
To become a real or a casual Christian

I'm not feeding the homeless
At no shelter or mission
That's not the position of a casual Christian

I'm not visiting no hospital with a gift basket and card
That would make my casual Christianity too hard

Thought:

Well let me help you while you're on your lil' mission
Their ain't no position in heaven for a casual Christian

DON'T DO IT

Don't preplace me
on where you think I should be
God said my gift would make room for me

Don't shut me out
'Cause you don't want me in
Don't look at me sideways
Because I've sinned

Don't replace me
'Cause you think I don't belong
Don't tell me to stop singing
'Cause you don't understand my songs

Don't tell me I'm not good enough
'Cause you don't know what I do
Don't tell me, I don't look good
Just 'cause I don't look like you

Don't close your ears to me
'Cause you can't relate to what I'm saying
Don't think your distractions
Will ever stop me from praying

Don't pre-judge me based on who you think I am

Don't do it!

Don't do it!

I'M SO TIRED

You: I'm so tired

God: Tired of what?

Praying?
Singing my praises?
Preaching my word?
Giving to the ministry?
Working in the field?
Living out my Word?
Or are you tired of...

All the other stuff you do?
Check your calendar, what is it filled with?

What have you done for me lately?

JUST PRAY!

Don't walk around and pace the floor
Don't raise your voice and slam the door
Don't say that you can't take no more

Just pray!

Don't have a fit, then fall out and scream
Don't let the enemy steal your dream
Don't try to figure out what the world means
Just pray!
Just pray!
Just pray!

CONSTRUCTION PAPER MASTERPIECE

My daughter gave me a masterpiece
That she drew with her tiny little hands

She used all the colors in her crayon box
To draw this lady and this man

She said, "This is my mommy and beside her is my dad
He is the best Father a girl could ever have"

I said to her softly, "Baby are you confused?"
You see her dad, she's never seen before
He drank a little too much booze

She said, "Oh no I'm not confused mommy, I see my dad
everyday
I talk to Him every morning, Every time I pray

He listens to my heart,
and answers all my requests
I asked Him to keep you strong,
So you'll be at your best

I told Him about how hard you worked
And how you cry at night when you're sad
He told me to let you know,
If you need him too. He will also be your Dad"

USE ME LORD, BUT NOT TODAY

Teach me Lord, but not today
Use me Lord, but don't make me pray

Search me Lord, but don't make me change
Fill me Lord, but don't make me strange

Challenge me Lord, but not too much strife
Consecrate me Lord, but don't change my life

Give me purpose Lord, but don't take my dream
Let me praise you Lord, but don't make me scream

Test me Lord, but in an easy way
Please, use me Lord

Just not today!

A LETTER FROM HELL

I wish I would have known
B 4 I left this place

But now I'm gone
Everything is so far away

I feel the pain that time could not erase
Now my soul is sentenced beyond time and space

All the opportunities of Your saving grace
Neglecting Your resurrection while you took my place

For me to be free and not experience this
Who is it, that says hell don't exist?

I was a fool cause I thought death was the end
But the pain of my rejection is my worst sin

Should have took heed
But I was consumed by my greed

Now it's plain to see
The reason you chose to bleed

Lord, forgive me please!

It took hell to bring me to my knees

Written by B. Sheldon

SHERÉA VÉJAUAN

Sheréa VéJauan is the author of the Coffee, Candlelight & Conversations with God, as well as several other titles, including, the 2017 Goals Journal, Realistically Speaking: Speaking What's Real, Keeping What's Holy, and many others. Sheréa resides in Southern California, devoted wife of twenty-five years to her husband Brian, and mother to their three children, Reginald, Jasmyn and Kennedy. http://shereavejauan.com/

More on Sherea VeJauan
Website: www.ShereaVeJauan.com
Twitter: www.twitter.com/vejauan
Facebook: www.facebook.com/vejauan

OUTSPOKEN

a collection of short stories, poems
and inspirational sayings inspired by
everyday life

Sheréa VéJauan

For additional copies of Outspoken! visit
http://shereavejauan.com/outspoken/ to order online.

www.ingramcontent.com/pod-product-compliance
Lightning Source LLC
Chambersburg PA
CBHW060511030426

42337CB00015B/1844